Chakras

A Beginner's Guide to Chakra Healing

Table of Contents

Introduction 1

Chapter 1: Step into the World of Chakras 3

Chapter 2: The Major Chakras 8

Chapter 3: Are your Chakras Balanced? 17

Chapter 4: Various Chakra States 25

Chapter 5: Repairing the Chakras 31

Chapter 6: Remedies for Chakras 44

Chapter 7: Taking Care of the Chakras 52

Chapter 8: Leveraging the Power of Meditation 64

Conclusion 71

Introduction

Do you constantly feel tired or drained? Do you want to change how you feel and replenish all this seemingly lost energy? Does it feel like something is holding you back from unlocking your inner potential? Do you want to get in touch with your inner spirituality? If you answered yes, then this is the perfect book for you. The answers to all your questions lie within the pages of this book.

What are chakras? Chakras are the energy centers present within your body along the length of your spine, starting at the base and going all the way to the crown of your head. Everything in this universe is made of energy. Energy can be neither created nor destroyed, but it can be transformed. This energy constantly moves and shifts from one thing to another, regardless of whether it is living or nonliving. The chakras present in your body help harness this universal energy, and are responsible for your physical, mental, emotional, and spiritual well-being.

Even though the chakra system originated in the East, several schools of thought support it across various religions. The concept of energy itself and universal energy is not new. Regardless of the name assigned to it, the idea of energy vibrating through the universe is quite real and accepted.

Harnessing your inner energy is important to discover and unlock your true potential. When the chakras are bright, open, and vibrant, they are filled with positive energy. On the other hand, if their energy is murky, blocked, or closed, we cannot function effectively or efficiently. Learning to balance and heal your chakras will improve your overall quality of life.

In this book, you'll learn about the meaning of chakras, their history, and the details of the major chakras. After this, you will learn to identify imbalances in the chakras, whether they are open or closed, and the importance of balancing them. Once you are armed with all this information, you'll learn how to balance and heal your chakras to optimize your overall quality of life. From meditation to visualization, simple techniques can be used to rebalance your chakras. All it takes is a little time, effort, and patience. Once you commit to healing them, you will notice a positive change in your life.

Chapter 1: Step into the World of Chakras

A popular belief is that different entities present in the universe are restricted to their physical forms. Well, this is nothing more than a misconception because the universe is made of energy. You may have come across this school of thought while studying science in school. Everything in the universe is made of matter. What is matter? It's a combination of different types of molecules. The next question is, what are molecules? When electrons and protons constantly collide with each other, they create energy that creates molecules. Everything in the universe, regardless of whether it is a living or nonliving thing, is made of this energy. This universal energy is present within and all around you. It is also known as subtle energy, and this energy flows through specific energy centers known as chakras, in the body.

What are Chakras?

In Sanskrit, a wheel or a disk is known as a chakra. Chakras are a part of your body, and they are known as the wheels of life. The spiritual and physiological elements present within your body interact with one another at these energy centers. The energy of the universe enters you through these chakras and flows out in the form of an aura surrounding you.

There are seven major and several minor chakras in your body. The major chakras correspond to different major organs starting at the base of the spine extending to the crown of your head. The minor chakras are associated with a bundle of nerves around these major organs. If these chakras are open and balanced, they function at their best. If their energy is blocked or not open, you experience imbalances or blockages in your physical and emotional well-being.

Once you start working on your chakras, you will become more self-aware. Healthy chakras help you to connect with the universal force of life, which your body uses to keep you happy and healthy. Tending to your body is your responsibility. It's not just your physical health that matters; taking care of other aspects of your life is equally important. A simple way to cater to your spiritual needs is by getting in touch with your chakras. Taking care of them and replenishing these energy centers keeps them vibrant and open. You will learn more about doing all this in the subsequent chapters.

History of Chakras

The concept of chakras originated in ancient India, and the first mention of chakras was discovered in the Upanishads. The Upanishads contain important instructions gathered from sacred Hindu scriptures known as Vedas. Vedas were compiled hundreds of years ago and are filled with important information and knowledge which is still applicable in the modern world. The rig Veda, Sama Veda, Atharva Veda, and Yajur Veda are the four Vedas. Unfortunately, no one knows the precise date when the Vedas were compiled. The only valuable piece of information is the Upanishads were compiled sometime around the 7th century. There are altogether 108 Upanishads, and 13 of them deal with chakras and information about them. The Upanishads include the Tantric concepts of chakras, mantras for activating them, their locations, and symbolism. Goraksha Satakam was written in the 10th century by Guru Goraknath and included information about awakening the chakras and meditating on them.

Sometime in the 16th century, the Sri Tattva Chintamani was composed by Swami Purannanda, and it included a chapter containing detailed descriptions and practices to activate and balance the chakras. This book also discussed the power associated with each of the chakras, and the movement of universal subtle energy in the body known as kundalini. Sir John

Woodroofe translated this literary work in the early part of the 20th century.

The theosophical movement was quite active at this time, and chakras were introduced to the West through Alice Bailey's works. During this theosophical movement, Charles Webster Leadbeater took the conventional concepts of Indian religious culture and Tantra and interpreted them freely to suit the sensibilities of the existing period. His influence on chakras cannot be ignored because his observations ultimately inspired a generation of clairvoyants. According to Tibetan rituals, chakras were considered a mental concept, whereas, in Hindu scripture, chakras were believed to be a source of spirituality. Leadbeater interpreted them from a clairvoyant perspective and implied that they are subtle bodies present within the human form with an independent objective. He considered them to be vortices of immense energy which connect your consciousness with the universal consciousness. He believed chakras help transform energy or consciousness. This is the standard interpretation of chakras followed by people today.

Until just a few decades ago, the concept of chakras was pretty much unheard of in the West. In the early '70s, "Nuclear evolution" was published by Christopher Hills. His work also influenced the western world to start thinking about chakras as much as Leadbeater's work did. An important area Hills concentrated on was the association of the seven chakras to the spectrum of color. The ancient tantric scriptures did not include this, but the association to the seven colors of the rainbow and chakras to personality traits have become part of mainstream chakra analysis.

Chapter 2: The Major Chakras

As mentioned in the previous chapter, there are seven major chakras in the body. These chakras correspond to different internal systems and body parts. The seven primary chakras affect you mentally, spiritually, emotionally, and physically. In this chapter, let's learn more about these chakras.

The Root Chakra

The Muladhara chakra, or the root chakra, is the first of the seven major chakras. It is located at the base of the spine. The Muladhara chakra is your source of usable physical energy and its physical manifestation. It is responsible for your feelings of safety and security. If these primary needs are not met, you cannot progress through life without worries. This chakra is the foundation for all aspects and qualities essential for your physical well-being.

The root chakra is associated with the color red and the element earth. It is a representation of your sense of being grounded and is the foundation for all the other chakras. The Muladhara chakra regulates any issues associated with your survival such as food, clothing, shelter, and finances. Your ability to smell and touch is also governed by it. Gemstones such as ruby, red jasper, bloodstone, garnet, red quartz, smoky quartz, and obsidian can be used to strengthen the energy of the root chakra.

Because of the chakra's physical location, it is responsible for your circulatory system, kidneys, bladder, adrenal glands, hips, rectum, feet, and legs. It is also responsible for your feeling of connectedness and staying grounded. You feel more grounded and confident even in the face of uncertainties when your root chakra is strong.

The Sacral Chakra

The Svadhisthana or sacral chakra is located in the lower abdominal region. It is associated with your ability to experience adventures and relate to those around you. It governs your sexuality, overall sense of well-being, pleasure, and a feeling of abundance. How you associate with others and experience and express your emotions are governed by this chakra. Its energy is associated with creativity and sexuality. You can interpret your life, others in it, and everything that happens around you by looking within yourself and tapping into the energy of the sacral chakra. It helps acknowledge the need for duality in nature. Whether it is the Chinese concept of yin and yang or the western philosophy of male and female counterparts, there needs to be balance. Without this balance, there will always be chaos.

Your ability to manage your finances, become creative, and achieve your goals becomes easier when the sacral chakra is active. It also removes any feelings of shame, guilt, or fear associated with your sexuality. This chakra governs your ability to taste and touch. It is related to the water element. The color it's associated with is orange. Different gemstones with orange hues such as carnelian, amber, and coral can be used to amplify the energy of the sacral chakra.

This chakra is located right below your navel and regulates your lower back, lymphatic system, large intestine, reproductive organs, kidneys, and bladder. When this chakra is functioning efficiently, your creativity increases, you are in touch with your inner sensuality, and you can concentrate on your personal enjoyment. On the other hand, it can also make you moody, manipulative, and cause you to live in denial when blocked or closed.

The Solar Plexus Chakra

The Manipur or the solar plexus chakra is located in the upper abdominal region. Your ability to control any situation, stay confident, and take risks is governed by this chakra. It is the seat of your sense of self-confidence, self-esteem, and self-worth. It helps improve your self-esteem and increases your sense of self.

It helps you live your life with integrity and honor while empowering others.

This chakra acts as the bridge between your emotional and mental energies. It ensures you not only listen to your heart but to your mind also. The color associated with it is yellow, and the natural element is fire. This chakra regulates your sense of sight and gut instincts. Wearing yellow gemstones such as orange quartz, tiger's eye, gold calcite, citrine, amber, and gold topaz help amplify this chakra's energy.

The solar plexus chakra is located roughly two inches above the navel, right below the sternum. Any trouble associated with the digestive system is due to an imbalance in the solar plexus chakra. It is associated with the pancreas, small intestine, gallbladder, liver, and stomach. If the energy of this chakra is balanced, you tend to live with respect and integrity. It increases your self-confidence and self-esteem. It also makes you self-disciplined, brave, courageous, and generous. You can live your life with ambition and make clear decisions to attain your goals when the solar plexus chakra is functioning as intended. On the other hand, your sense of identity, self-esteem, self-confidence, and self-discipline take a back seat if its energy is imbalanced. It can also make you seem narcissistic to a certain extent if out of balance.

The Heart Chakra

As the name suggests, the Anahata chakra, or the heart chakra, is located in the chest cavity. As is obvious from the name, this chakra deals with everything associated with the heart. It is representative of healing, happiness, love, and peace. It concentrates on feelings of compassion, love, and forgiveness. Because it is located at the center of your body, it concentrates on love as the primary basis for life. Any emotional pain you experience causes changes in the energy of this chakra. Remember that all of the positive feelings provided by the chakra should not only be shared with others, but with yourself too. Unless you are compassionate, loving, kind, and forgiving toward yourself, you cannot make peace with anything else in life. If you cannot love yourself, you can never truly love anyone else. This chakra helps you understand that true happiness stems from within, and the key to living a happy life lies in your hands.

The location of this chakra means it is responsible for regulating the functions of the respiratory system including the heart, diaphragm, and lungs. If you experience any problems associated with these body parts, chances are it's due to an imbalance in the Anahata chakra's energy. This chakra is associated with the colors pink and green, and your sense of touch. The element of the heart chakra is air. Wearing pink or green colored gemstones such as emerald, jade, rose quartz, tourmaline, moss agate, malachite, and aventurine helps tap into the healing power of the heart chakra.

The Throat Chakra

The Vishuddha or the throat chakra is located at the base of your throat and is associated with your ability to communicate clearly, effectively, and efficiently. It is the seat of your self-expression. Self-expression is not restricted to communication and includes your ability to speak up for yourself too. It is responsible for your feelings of creativity and the willpower required to make healthy choices. The energy of this chakra helps you to live your life with personal honor and integrity.

This chakra is quite similar to a teacher who is opening up and sharing their wisdom with others. It not only helps communicate your thoughts and emotions but is also your spirit's mouthpiece for communication too. This is where your soul's expression truly lies. The color associated with it is blue, and it regulates your sense of smell and hearing. Apart from that, this chakra also regulates your ability to communicate. When the throat chakra is functioning efficiently, you become adept at self-expression. You can communicate without any confusion or ambiguity. It helps you to express your inner desires and feelings or emotions. On the other hand, you can become quite critical of yourself and others, and become a poor listener if there are any imbalances in this chakra.

Any blue-colored gemstones will help enhance the energy of this chakra. Some gemstones you can use are lapis lazuli, aquamarine, turquoise, amazonite, and sodalite. Blue is also the color of self-confidence and expression. The element this chakra is associated with is ether, or space.

The Third Eye Chakra

The Ajna or the third eye chakra is located between the eyes on your forehead. It is also known as the brow chakra due to its location. It is believed to be your seat of integration and wisdom. Your collective intellect, visions, and ability to listen to your gut are regulated by it. This is one of the higher chakras that connect the physical realm with the spiritual one. The higher chakras usually regulate all the senses associated with the lower chakras. So, this third eye chakra is responsible for all your senses. When the energy of the chakra is well balanced, it becomes easier to align yourself with the powers you don't see, such as the cosmic energy. It also makes you more sensitive to sounds, motion, and other happenings.

The color associated with chakra is indigo, or violet. The element it is associated with is cosmic energy, or light. Different gemstones you can use to enhance the power of this chakra are lapis lazuli and fluoride. The spiritual energy of this chakra helps you to get in touch with yourself without any reservations. It regulates your pituitary glands, all the sensory organs, nervous system, head, and brain. It also regulates your skull and eyes. If you experience constant headaches or struggle to maintain clarity of thought, it can be due to imbalances in this chakra.

The third eye chakra also governs your power of imagination. If you are bored, uninterested, are extremely critical and judgmental of yourself and others, and your imagination has taken a backseat, it can be due to imbalances or blockages in the third eye chakra.

The Crown Chakra

The final chakra is the crown chakra which is located at the top of your head. It is also known as the Sahasrara. It is the most spiritual of all chakras and is deeply connected with your spirituality. It helps bring together inner and outer beauty to create a sense of peace and oneness with oneself and the universe. It connects you to higher dimensions and is the key to attaining enlightenment. This is the most important of all chakras and it is the highest one. The colors associated with it are white, purple, or gold. If this chakra is active, you are spiritually aware and can live in the moment without getting bogged down by the emotional baggage of the past or worries about the future. The best gemstones you can use to heal and balance the energy of the chakra are clear quartz and selenite. If this chakra is not functioning as intended, it can make you materialistic, dogmatic, and disinterested in life.

Chapter 3: Are your Chakras Balanced?

Have there been any instances where you felt physically and mentally affected by something but could not put your finger on the exact reason? Chances are those instances are a manifestation of imbalances in your chakras. In this section, you will learn how to identify imbalances in the different chakras.

Identifying Imbalances in Chakras

The Root Chakra

As previously mentioned, the root chakra is located at the base of your spine, quite close to the tailbone. When its energy is imbalanced, your legs are affected. It also harms your immune function. It's believed that imbalances in this chakra harm women more than men. Constipation is a common physical manifestation of an imbalance in this chakra. Since the root chakra is associated with your adrenal glands, your fight or flight response is regulated by it. An imbalance in the root chakra also directly results in dysregulated emotional responses. This chakra is associated with your sense of security and safety. If you don't feel comfortable within your own skin, it can be due to an imbalance in this chakra. If your home life feels a little unsettled and chaotic, your sense of security is challenged, and you feel stuck in life, these are all signs of an imbalanced root chakra. You might also experience pain and stiffness in your legs and feet, a reduction in physical stability, and a sense of insecurity.

The Sacral Chakra

This chakra is located at the sacrum and is associated with your sex organs. It is associated with your emotions and sense of creativity. The sacral chakra also governs your one-on-one relationships and level of intimacy. Any imbalances in this chakra can make you feel out of touch with your emotions. If you're struggling to deal with your emotions, get in touch with your inner self, or are feeling closed off, it's time to rebalance the sacral chakra. When the sacral chakra is imbalanced, you may also feel emotionally overwhelmed at the slightest of happenings, have a lack of creativity and imagination, and a general feeling of being closed off. It also triggers reproductive and sexual issues, reduces your sex drive, and causes pain or stiffness in the hips and lower back.

The Solar Plexus Chakra

This chakra is located at your abdomen and is associated with your self-confidence. The solar plexus chakra governs all thoughts, feelings, and opinions about yourself. It essentially determines the relationship you share with yourself. Because it is located near the abdomen, you can experience abdominal pain and digestive troubles if the solar plexus chakra is imbalanced. Any imbalances in its energy can reduce your self-esteem, overinflate your ego, and make it difficult to feel good about yourself. Any inability to commit or follow through on your goals is also associated with an imbalanced solar plexus chakra.

The Heart Chakra

The heart chakra is located in your chest cavity and affects your chest, shoulders, hands, arm, and upper back region. This chakra is responsible for love. It's not just the love you feel for others, but for yourself too. The ability to forgive, be kind and compassionate toward others, and give and receive love are governed by the heart chakra. Since it is located in your chest cavity, any pain in the upper back or chest can be due to an imbalanced heart chakra. It can also manifest as tightness and tension in the shoulders and general upper back pain. The inability to receive love is also due to an imbalanced heart chakra. You may experience a lack of compassion toward others and yourself and feel a sense of loss in terms of love. Your love life can be severely harmed by the imbalances of energy in the heart chakra.

The Throat Chakra

As the name suggests, the throat chakra is located at the base of your throat and governs your neck, throat, jaw, mouth, and ears. It is the seat of your self-expression, communication, and expression of identity. When to use your voice or stay quiet, these actions are both governed by this chakra. It helps you speak from the heart and mind while listening with compassion and empathy. You may experience laryngitis and a sore throat if there are imbalances in this chakra. Another physical manifestation you need to watch out for is any pain or stiffness in the neck, pain in the neck or jaw, or the habit of excessively grinding your teeth. If you are struggling with not knowing when to stay quiet or are used to talking all the time, it can be due to an imbalanced throat chakra. Similarly, if you are experiencing trouble speaking up for yourself, standing by your thoughts and ideas, or expressing yourself without any difficulties, it's all due to an imbalanced throat chakra. The inability to set boundaries or respect them is also a psychological manifestation of imbalanced throat chakra energy.

The Third Eye Chakra

This chakra is located at the center of your forehead and is associated with your gut instinct, inner wisdom, intuition, and imagination. This chakra governs your ability to look deep within your heart and get in touch with the parts of yourself that are often ignored. It essentially lets you see the big picture without getting bogged down by the troubles of daily life. It helps you maintain an optimistic outlook about life and the future in general. When this chakra is imbalanced, your intuition takes a backseat. You might experience headaches and brain fog which prevents you from making good decisions. Your imagination either becomes inactive or overactive to the extent you are constantly lost in an imaginary world or are daydreaming. Imbalances in this chakra also reduce your inspiration and prevent you from trusting your intuition.

The Crown Chakra

The crown chakra is located at the top of your skull and is associated with the sense of enlightenment. It helps you understand that you are a small part of the universal consciousness. It helps you determine where you stand in this world and gives you a sense of purpose. The physical manifestation of any imbalances in this chakra present themselves as headaches. If you are struggling to concentrate, your attention span has gone down, and you are unable to focus on a given task, it can be due to imbalances in this chakra. It also prevents you from being an empathetic listener or seeing things from someone else's perspective. It makes you narrow-minded and prevents you from truly understanding the role you play in the universe. The inability to see beyond your own small world is due to an imbalanced crown chakra.

Balancing the Chakras

If the energy radiating from different chakras is blocked, it will hamper the quality of your life. From physical and mental to emotional and spiritual health, all these aspects are significantly affected by the energy of chakras. In the previous section, you were introduced to different difficulties you might face if there are imbalances in any of the seven chakras. An important point to remember is that an imbalance in one chakra can cause an imbalance in other chakras.

By balancing the chakras, the first advantage you stand to gain is that your body functions the way it is supposed to. All the major chakras are responsible for regulating the function of important organs, and nerve bundles around them. Unless all internal organs and systems function efficiently, your health cannot be maintained. You can ensure there is internal harmony by concentrating on balancing your chakras. The various physical manifestations of imbalances in chakras were discussed in the previous section. If you notice any of them, it is time to concentrate on internal chakra healing.

When all your chakras are open, spinning vibrantly, and working in harmony with each other, your emotional and mental stability increases. It not only makes you more aware of your emotions, but of those around you as well. Your empathy, compassion, and the ability to give and receive love are all governed by chakras. By balancing them, you can ensure all your emotional and mental needs are taken care of. Since these needs form the basis of any relationship you develop in life, taking care of your chakras is important.

The energy of open and balanced chakras creates a positive outlook towards life, gives you a better perception of behavior, and makes you more aware of your own thought process. This self-awareness goes a long way toward fixing any negative thinking patterns and replacing them with positive ones.

The previous section mentioned the solar plexus chakra as the seat of your self-confidence and self-esteem. If this chakra's energy is open and balanced, you will see an improvement in both these aspects of your life. Remember, all these benefits are associated with open and vibrant chakras in the active phase and not the overactive one. You will learn more about the stages of different chakras in the next chapter.

Balancing the chakras will enhance your creativity, improve your perception of resourcefulness, and make you more open to change. It also enhances your ability to concentrate, memorize, and be open to all the different life experiences. A combination of these factors is important to learn, grow, and develop in life. Balancing the chakras is also vital for your physical health, and therefore, when all the chakras are well balanced, your ability to stay healthy and free of illness will increase. Apart from all this, the energy from these chakras will make you more energetic than ever before.

Chapter 4: Various Chakra States

You may be quite eager to learn about balancing the chakras after reading about the benefits that doing so offers. Before you get into this, it is important to understand the different states in which chakras usually exist.

Conditions of the Chakras

We learned earlier that chakras are known as the wheels of life. When the chakras are spinning vibrantly, they are full of light. As with everything else in life, the state the chakras are in is not fixed. Instead, they keep shifting from one state to another depending on the circumstances you are experiencing. To avoid any problems in the future and to ensure their light does not fade, it's important to understand the ideal conditions of chakras. This will give you a better understanding of how energy flows in your body. Since chakras are the energy vertices, the light around them is usually swirling. These vertices are found at seven parts of your body where the major chakras lie.

Understanding the state of your chakras is essential. Unless you can identify the chakra's current state, you cannot determine the ideal healing technique. Chakras usually exist in an open state, blocked state, sealed, and a healing or a balanced state.

Let us look in detail at all these states:

The Open State

In their open state, the chakras are open to absorbing the energy they need to balance themselves. Unless the chakra is open, you cannot heal or balance it. When open, the energy flows freely to and from the chakra. From the external environment to the chakras located in your body, the energy will be able to flow without any obstructions.

The Blocked State

As the name suggests, in this state, the energy in the chakra is blocked. The energy around them needs to be swirling, and when blocked, the light around them stops spinning. Instead, it can start to rotate in the opposite direction. If one chakra is blocked, you will realize the energy of the other chakras will also become blocked. Since all the chakras are interconnected, an imbalance in one usually results in imbalances in others too. Think of an energy blockage as a traffic jam. Unless the traffic jam is cleared, there is no free flow. While healing chakras, you use the energy present within the chakra and the universal energy to heal it. If the chakra itself is blocked, this energy is blocked too.

The Sealed State

Every chakra has a layer of energy around it, like a protective shield. When you think of shields, you might think of body armor and medieval knights. The shield around the chakra performs a similar function, which is to ensure the chakra's energy is confined to it and it is not absorbing any negative energy from the surroundings. As mentioned, energy is flowing freely in nature, and it moves from one thing to another. Whether it is positive or negative, the energy keeps flowing, so, it is important to protect your chakras from the undesirable energies. The shield around it does this. This also helps the chakras perform their functions efficiently. After you complete reenergizing or healing your chakras, it is important to seal them. If not, they may attract negative energy and fall out of balance.

The Healing Or The Balanced State

The chakras are in this state once they are fully healed from the inside. Their energy becomes bright and vibrant once they're healed. It also means their energy starts flowing freely through the chakras, and they start spinning in the right direction instead of the wrong one. When they are healed, you will realize these chakras don't need any other external energy to keep going. Instead, the energy present within is sufficient to guide them. The direction in which chakras spin is clockwise. If the chakras are healed and functioning well, they move in a clockwise direction and the opposite when they are imbalanced.

Various Phases of the Chakras

Chakras not only exist in different states, but they also go through different phases. These phases of the chakras are usually based on the energy present in the chakra. There are four phases for each chakra, and they are the active, underactive, overactive, and passive phases. Determining the phase of the chakra helps you choose the best technique to heal it and decide the kind of energy it needs.

Active Phase

As the name suggests, in this stage, the chakras are quite active and vibrant. This is the ideal state for any chakra to exist in. It means the chakras are functioning optimally, like they're supposed to. For instance, if the root chakra is in an active phase, it means your fight or flight responses are regulated. If this instinct functions properly, you can make better decisions under challenging circumstances. During the active stage, your body is mentally, emotionally, physically, and spiritually healthy. All the energies are spinning vibrantly and brightly without any blockages.

Passive Phase

When you are at peace with yourself and your body is at ease, the chakras are at peace. During the passive stage, the chakras are essentially taking a break from all their work and recuperating. Think of it as a much-needed weekend away from work. This stage occurs when the energy both inside and outside of you are in complete balance. It is the representation of homeostasis.

Underactive Phase

When your chakra is going through an underactive phase, it's quite similar to a silent kid in a classroom. For him to start working with others and mingle with his peers, he needs a slight push. Similarly, your chakras from time to time will need a little push to revitalize themselves and start spinning vibrantly. Challenging circumstances and the inability to cope with them properly can drain your energy. If this happens, the energy from your chakras also reduces. Also, chakras are underactive when their energy is not utilized.

Overactive Phase

As the name suggests, in this state, the energy of the chakras is sent into overdrive. This is the phase chakras are in when you feel extremely emotional, or your emotions are running high. The same thing happens when you feel overwhelmed. The energy of the chakras is quite sensitive to all that's happening in and around you. As mentioned, chakras are magnets for energy. If the energies around are quite overwhelming, the chakras get overwhelmed. This, in turn, results in imbalances of the chakras with physical, emotional, and mental manifestations.

Chapter 5: Repairing the Chakras

Now that you know the signs and symptoms of imbalances and blockages in the chakras, the next step is to repair them. Repairing chakras is quite easy, and most of the suggestions discussed in this chapter are important to lead a healthy and happy life. Remember, repairing and healing the chakras is not a one-time process. Instead, it is a culmination of small steps taken daily.

The Root Chakra

Fear is the primary challenge you need to overcome to heal and repair this chakra. Developing courage and realizing your true purpose in life will help tackle this. By understanding that you are meant to do bigger and better things in life, the fear of trivial things goes away. Fear is also a common factor that prevents people from taking the steps required to attain their goals. Here are some simple suggestions you can use to repair the energy of the root chakra:

Spend some time outdoors and get away from the daily stress of life. Walking barefoot helps reduce any stress and increases the grounding effect by harnessing the earth's healing powers. The root chakra is responsible for your sense of safety, security, and belongingness. Hugging someone, especially someone you love, can make you feel grounded and calm. You can also concentrate on the chakra's physical location and rub your lower back to reduce any stress present there.

Add some plants to your surroundings to increase your connection with Mother Earth. Concentrate on understanding your needs and wants. Believe that you have the power required to manifest them into reality. When it comes to repairing chakras, never underestimate the power of positive affirmations. An affirmation is a sentence you believe in. Positive affirmations are positive sentences that help rewire your subconscious and turn it into something more positive and desirable. You can create your positive affirmations and repeat them to attain a specific goal or need.

Here are some positive affirmations you can use to further enhance the energy of this chakra:

- I am safe, secure, and protected.

- I am connected to my body and grounded in the present.

- I feel peaceful, and I am a being of divine energy.

- I stand for my values, justice, and truth.

- I have a bigger purpose on this Earth, and I will serve it.

- I love myself and trust the decisions I make.

- I believe the choices I make will help me grow and transform as an individual.

The Sacral Chakra

The sacral chakra is your body's pleasure and passion center. The primary obstacles you need to deal with here are taking risks and avoiding any feelings of shame and guilt. Practice aromatherapy to repair the energy of this chakra. Lighting incense sticks or scented candles helps to calm your senses and renew the energy of this chakra. Another simple way to relax is by getting a massage. Massage not only reduces any physical tension in your body but also calms your mind and regulates your emotions too. Take a leisurely bath using Epsom salts to cleanse any negative energy within and around you.

Start feeling all the different vibrations around you and attune your sense of sight and sound to connect with the universe. Feel the energy around you and let it flow freely through your body. To eliminate negative energy around you, clean your house, and spend some time with your loved ones. Start honoring your body and respecting it to repair the energies of this chakra.

Some positive affirmations you can use to tap into the power of this chakra are as follows:

- I love, cherish, and respect my body.

- I've healthy boundaries, and I respect them.

- I appreciate everything going on in my life, and I'm living in the moment.

- I respect and value myself and my body.

- I'm not scared of experiencing pleasure, and I'm open to it.

- I am using my senses to live my life to the fullest.

- I'm not scared of my sexuality, and I accept and cherish it.

The Solar Plexus Chakra

The main challenge associated with this chakra is a lack of self-confidence and an inability to understand your own power. Understand that you are the only one in control of your life, and no one else can take this power away from you. Regardless of all that happens, you have complete control over your reactions and responses. To protect the energy of your solar plexus chakra, become aware of any negative thoughts and self-talk. Replace negative with positive feelings by using positive affirmations.

Instead of ignoring your anger and other powerful feelings, acknowledge and accept them. Once you accept them, you can channel them positively and constructively without causing any harm. If you are struggling to understand others, put yourself in their shoes and try to view things from their perspective. Realize that you have a higher purpose and mission in this life. Doing this adds more depth to your individuality and makes you aware of everything you do.

Leverage the power of positive affirmations to strengthen your solar plexus chakra. Here are some suggestions you can use:

- I choose to be the best version of myself.

- I accept and love myself.

- I am capable of achieving greatness, and I can achieve my goals.

- I am proud of my achievements.

- I have the power to choose in any situation.

- I feel my power and accept it.

- I'm looking for opportunities to grow.

- I'm not scared of taking risks or facing challenges.

- I know I have the power to overcome any obstacles in life.

- Everything I experience is a learning opportunity, and I acknowledge this.

The Heart Chakra

The Anahata chakra helps you get through life, get in touch with your inner self, and appreciate everything that happens to you. Naturally, the biggest challenge it faces is grief. By opening yourself to love, giving and receiving, you can repair the energy of this chakra. Remember, love is a two-way street. You can't always be a giver or a receiver. Any imbalance in this equation is not good for the heart chakra. The first step toward love is to love yourself. Unless you are capable of loving yourself unconditionally, you cannot give or receive it.

Start by accepting and acknowledging yourself the way you are. Despite all your flaws, concentrate on loving yourself. It's quite easy to be harsh and critical. Instead of engaging in criticism, concentrate on the positive aspects. Why don't you write a love letter to yourself? Make a note of all your achievements, positive traits, and everything good about yourself. Engaging in a little self-appreciation from time to time can work wonders for your self-esteem and confidence.

If you have made any mistakes, accept them and take responsibility for them. Unless you learn from your mistakes, you are bound to repeat them. Remember, you are your worst critic. If you are unnecessarily harsh on yourself, it merely worsens how you feel. If your loved one comes to you in times of need or they have made a mistake, how will you react? If you respond with compassion and love, it's time to channel these emotions toward yourself.

Start spending more time with your loved ones. Whether it is your friends, family members, or anyone else, spending time with those who lift your spirits is good for your heart. Start by expressing love for others. Love doesn't always have romantic undertones. It can be affection towards siblings and parents, a family pet, or anything else. If you love something about a person in your life, tell them.

Another way to express and accept love is by practicing gratitude. Give thanks for everything good in your life. If you now have something that you once hoped for, now is the time to be grateful. Whether it is a hot meal, the loving company of your friends and family, or your job, these are all things to be grateful for. When you express gratitude, you send positive vibrations to the universe that attract more positivity into your life.

Here are a few positive affirmations that you can practice daily to unleash the true potential of your heart chakra:

- I acknowledge, accept, and love myself the way I am.
- I am open to giving and receiving love.
- I accept things despite any flaws.
- I am in touch with my inner child, and I love life.

- I not only forgive those who have wronged me, but also myself for the mistakes I made.

- I'm loved, wanted, accepted, and understood the way I am.

- I am open to kindness, compassion, and positivity.

- I am grateful for all my life experiences.

The Throat Chakra

The throat chakra is one of the first spiritual chakras. It inspires your creativity and self-expression. If you are honest with yourself and can communicate without ambiguity, it is due to this chakra. If you are unable to express yourself, are used to lying, or are unable to see the truth, it can be due to imbalances in this chakra. The good news is you can work on improving all of this.

Start your day with a positive affirmation to ensure that positive energy stays with you. Never underestimate the power of the law of attraction. This law is based on the assumption that like attracts like. If you give positive energy, you are attracting more positivity in your life, and negativity attracts more negativity. Instead of concentrating on everything that's lacking or missing, concentrate on the good. By starting your day with gratitude, you are welcoming more positivity. As you go about your day, expect that good things will happen instead of worrying about everything that can go wrong.

Close your eyes and engage your sense of hearing. Concentrate on all the noises and sounds you can hear and nothing else. This simple exercise ensures you are living in the moment and not getting bogged down by everything else. Avoid complaining about others or yourself. Make it a daily habit. Since the throat chakra is associated with your throat, engaging your vocal cords is a good idea. Regardless of whether you are a good singer or not, try singing! This also reduces any negative emotions you are experiencing while filling you with positivity. You might also like to concentrate on learning a new language. If there is a language you have been meaning to learn, now is the time to work on it. This engages the energy of the throat chakra.

To improve your ability to communicate, practice what you want to say before you speak. While communicating, ensure you are expressing yourself without any bias or apprehensions. Make it a point to communicate your ideas, thoughts, feelings, and emotions without any ambiguity. Apart from speaking, you need to develop good listening skills too. Communication is a combination of both listening and speaking. Learning to speak up for yourself also enhances the power of this chakra. Similarly, learn when not to speak. At times, silence is precious, and listening can do a lot of good.

You can use the following affirmations to enhance the power of your throat chakra:

- I live my life with integrity and honesty.
- I can communicate my thoughts, ideas, and feelings without any trouble.
- I am communicating honestly, openly, and clearly.
- I am living an authentic life.
- I am nourishing my spirit through creativity.
- I'm taking good care of myself.
- I speak my truth and listen to the same.
- I know when it is time to listen, and I do not deny it.

The Third Eye Chakra

The third eye chakra helps connect your inner and outer worlds through spirituality. If you get too caught up in only one of these realms, it takes away your ability to live in the real world. The lines between reality and fiction can get blurred if the energy of this chakra is not balanced. To heal this chakra, you need to live in the real world while using your imagination, without getting caught up in the fantasy realm.

Engage in activities that promote your creativity and imagination. Whether it is watching movies, engaging in artwork, or any other hobby; exercise your creativity. Exercising your creative muscles is also good for your emotional and mental well-being. If you are unsure about a specific hobby, there is no time like the present to start learning something new. A simple way to increase the power of this chakra is by trusting your intuition. Keep yourself open to the guidance you are constantly receiving from the universe and listen to it. Don't forget to thank the cosmic energy for the guidance and help it is sending your way.

Use these affirmations for tapping into the potential of your third eye chakra:

- I trust my intuition and welcome it.

- I know my truth, and I believe it.

- I am connected with universal energy, and I'm open to learning from it.

- I am intuitive, and I trust my intuition.

- I listen to my inner guide and trust its wisdom.

- I am at peace with myself.

- I love, accept, and forgive myself.

- Every mistake I've made is a lesson I've learned, and I am moving in the right direction.

The Crown Chakra

When the crown chakra is vibrant, you become selfless and are at peace with everything happening in and around you. Dealing with your sense of attachment is the primary problem associated with this chakra. Learn to understand that everything changes, and nothing can ever be constant. Instead of getting attached to materialistic possessions, learn to see the big picture. Things and people come and go from life. Letting go of worldly attachments helps you to connect with your inner spirituality. Accept change and do not deny or resist it.

Concentrate on getting in touch with your inner spirituality. Regardless of your religious beliefs, open up your body, mind, and soul to the energy of the cosmos. After all, you are but a small being in the vast universe. Accepting this brings with it a sense of peace and liberation. Listening to classical music, engaging in philanthropic activities, and meditating are simple ways to get in touch with your spiritual self.

Here are some affirmations you can use to manifest the healing energy of the crown chakra:

- I am at peace with myself and the world.

- I am grateful for everything good in my life.

- I'm grateful for all my experiences.

- I honor the cosmic energy within me, and I am a part of it.

- I cherish my spirit and respect it.

- I am trying to understand and learn from my past experiences to grow as an individual.

- I am connected with myself and the universe.

- I accept and love myself.

- I am living in the present moment.

- I am letting go of all worldly possessions.

Chapter 6: Remedies for Chakras

Remedying any imbalances or blockages in chakras is possible with a little conscious effort, consistency, and patience. You can use music, colors, aromas, and crystals to achieve this goal.

Listen to Music

Have you ever noticed how different songs affect you? For instance, a peppy number can make you feel upbeat, while a sad song can bring up sad memories. Now, it's time to leverage the power of music to heal your chakras. Energy has different vibrations, and the vibrations of music can be used for restoring the chakras. You can also use music while meditating to improve the overall effect of the session. Different genres of music can stimulate the energy of chakras. For instance, classical or relaxing music helps shift your focus from stress to something more pleasant.

You can renew the solar plexus chakra's energy by listening to music that invigorates and inspires you. You will realize you have some songs you usually listen to that make you feel inspired and motivated. By channeling the motivational or inspirational energy of a song, you are healing the solar plexus chakra.

The heart chakra is your center of love and inner peace. Any music that calms and relaxes you can be used for healing the heart chakra. Calming and relaxing music doesn't necessarily have to be soft. It just needs to have a relaxing effect on you. Any song that stimulates your imagination for creativity will help balance the energy of the throat chakra. You can also use music to reenergize this chakra. If a song inspires your self-esteem, it can be used for strengthening the throat chakra.

Listening to ethereal music can help you to focus on your spiritual chakras. The two chakras that benefit from such music are the crown and the third eye chakra. While using music, you need to keep an open mind to the music you are listening to. Don't judge your choices. As long as the music makes you feel good, go with it.

Work with Colors

All the chakras are associated with different colors. By incorporating these colors into your daily life, you can heal them and improve their energy. At times, you may have noticed that you have a sudden urge to wear a specific color. This is nothing more than your chakra telling you it needs a little boost. Open your closet and see the color that dominates your collection. You may not have thought about it, but your favorite color also corresponds with one of the chakras. The notion of deciding or choosing a favorite color is more significant than you probably believed. For instance, powerful personalities often wear red. The question is, why is red considered to be a power color? If you take a moment and think about the chakras and their corresponding colors, it all becomes clear.

As mentioned earlier, the root chakra is associated with red. The root chakra is the seat of primal energy, and therefore, red is associated with this energy. The sacral chakra is associated with orange, which stimulates feelings of pleasure and happiness. It is a positive color and is quite warm. Another positive and warm color is yellow, and it is associated with the solar plexus chakra. It helps to improve your creativity and symbolizes pleasure. Yellow is also believed to symbolize abundance and vitality. The color associated with the heart chakra is green or pink. These soothing colors are best suited for healing as well as meditation. The throat chakra is associated with different shades of blue, which have a soothing and calming effect on the wearer. It is also the spiritual color of healing. The third eye chakra is associated with dark hues of blue or indigo which is the color of spirituality and wisdom. So, wearing indigo brings with it a sense of clarity. The crown chakra is associated with white or violet. It is believed these colors keep all negative energy at bay and make the wearer feel calm and relaxed.

Start experimenting with different colors and notice how your chakras behave when you wear a specific color. Also, use these colors while awakening or balancing the energy of a specific chakra. For instance, on the days when you need to feel more confident than usual, opt for yellow. Similarly, if you are experiencing any troubles in your relationships, wearing green or pink can help.

Leverage the Power of Crystals

To reduce any imbalances within a chakra and increase its energy, you can use crystals and stones. You might have heard about stones with healing powers or properties. Now that you are aware of the different colors associated with the chakras, it's time to incorporate stones and crystals of corresponding colors to work with your chakras. Whether the gemstones are incorporated into a piece of jewelry or you prefer to carry them with you, the stones' positive vibrations have a healing effect on the chakras.

Garnet, ruby, red jasper, hematite, onyx, and black tourmaline are all associated with the root chakra. Garnet helps eliminate negativity and cope with any issues associated with love and devotion. It also brings with it a sense of stability and commitment, while ruby is a protective stone with a positive aura. It also has a positive effect on matters related to love, spirituality, and finances. If you want to feel relaxed and grounded, opt for hematite.

Carnelian, citrine, yellow jasper, orange zincate, and orange calcite are associated with the sacral chakra. Carnelian helps rationalize overwhelming fears, anger, and rage. It eliminates these negative emotions and replaces them with assurance and inner peace. Another positive stone is citrine, which can make you feel happy and radiates positive energy. Yellow jasper is a protective stone that drives away any negative feelings and fills you with protective warmth while increasing your awareness.

The different stones you can use to rebalance the solar plexus chakra's energy are yellow sapphire, yellow calcite, and amber. All these crystals are in different shades of yellow and help rebalance the energy of the solar plexus chakra while increasing your self-confidence and self-esteem. If you are struggling to believe in yourself, the warmth and reassuring energy of these yellow stones will help.

Rose quartz, tourmaline, malachite, jade, and aventurine are associated with the heart chakra. Rose quartz is believed to have healing properties that magnify positive emotions associated with happiness, love, and peace. Your self-confidence and inspiration increase when you use tourmaline, while malachite brings with it spirituality and maturity. Your self-confidence can also increase along with peace and harmony by wearing jade.

Turquoise, Angelite, sodalite, and blue calcite are the preferred crystals for the throat chakra. Turquoise has a positive effect on the wearer and is believed to increase your sense of inner peace while improving your strength. Sodalite is associated with honesty and logical thinking.

Lapis lazuli and sapphire are well suited for the third eye chakra. They are protective stones that help harness your creative energies while bringing with them a sense of the wisdom of the universe. They are also associated with beauty and are believed to represent prosperity.

Amethyst, diamond, and clear quartz are associated with the crown chakra. The calming effect of amethyst is believed to fill the wearer with strength and stability. It also brings with it a sense of peace and commitment. Diamond is representative of abundance and perfection, while clear quartz has calming effects.

If you are hesitant about trying crystals or unsure which ones to use, opt for clear quartz. The energy of this crystal can be used to heal imbalances in all of the chakras. You can incorporate these specific stones and crystals into an amulet, jewelry you wear daily, or even place them close to your bed while sleeping. Alternatively, the simple act of carrying these stones with you in your wallet or handbag also helps. The idea is to ensure the energy vibrations from the crystals and stones are flowing into your body.

Use Aromatherapy

Apart from using sounds and colors to cleanse and heal your chakras, you can use fragrances to stimulate your chakras. Any activity that stimulates your senses can be used for chakras too. Just because the chakras are representative of your nonphysical body does not mean they are separate from your physical body. So, using the physical senses goes a long way toward healing your chakras. One of the strongest senses is the sense of smell. It is quite powerful and is associated with your imagination and memories. Does a specific scent remind you of an incident? For instance, the smell of cookies may remind you of your grandmother's home! Memories are quite powerful, and our senses regulate them. By leveraging your sense of smell, you can work with your chakras.

Start using essential oils to connect and heal your chakras. Burning essential oils is an inexpensive yet effective way to attain this goal. As with colors and crystals, chakras are associated with different fragrances too.

The root chakra will benefit from patchouli and frankincense fragrances, while orange, clove, and juniper are associated with the sacral chakra. Lemon and rosemary work well for the solar plexus chakra. Rose, rosewood, and basil are the aromas associated with the heart chakra. The fragrance of sage, blue chamomile, and lemongrass benefits the throat chakra, while spruce, lavender, and clary sage are associated with the third eye chakra. Use myrrh, geranium, and sandalwood to rebalance the energies of the crown chakra.

Chapter 7: Taking Care of the Chakras

As mentioned, energy is the basis of the universe. This energy lives within us and is a gift we have received from the divine powers of creation. Whether you are religious or not, spirituality is something different. Chakras are a part of your spiritual energy system. Spiritual energy affects your physical energy too. Unless the energy centers are vibrant and spinning brightly and there is a healthy flow of energy on the inside, you cannot function effectively or efficiently.

Tips to Help Your Chakras

Think of chakras as your smartphone. At the end of the day, the battery is drained, and you need to recharge the phone to use it again. Similarly, the chakras need to be charged from time to time to ensure they function efficiently. In this section, let's look at some simple techniques you can use to recharge and boost the energy of the seven major chakras in your body.

Reconnecting With The Earth

Most of us live in concrete jungles and are often confined to the four walls of our houses and workplace. If you want to rebalance the energy of chakras and give them the additional support required to function efficiently, you need to take a break from this routine. You must spend some time outdoors. Spending time in nature not only relaxes you but helps reconnect with its healing energies as well. Ideally, walking barefoot in the grass is good for recharging the root chakra's energy. The root chakra is associated with grounding energy, and what is more grounding than the earth? This helps you get in touch with nature and absorb its healing energies. By grounding yourself and living in the present, you are strengthening the feeling of security and safety, which automatically strengthens the root chakra.

Water Washes Away Impurities

We all bathe daily, but why do we do this? We do this to get rid of all impurities our bodies collect throughout the day. Water has a cleansing and detoxifying effect and washes away all impurities. Adding a little sea salt to your daily bathwater helps cleanse any impurities associated with the sacral chakra. Taking a dip in the ocean is perhaps the best way to cleanse its energy and add some positivity to the sacral chakra. While bathing, visualize that all the issues associated with this chakra, such as sexual troubles, guilt, and shame are being washed away by the water.

Add Physical Movement

Exercising regularly is important. This is one of the fundamental aspects of health you must not ignore. Even exercising for as little as 20-30 minutes a day can positively affect your mental and physical health. While you exercise, feel-good hormones known as endorphins are released by your body. This automatically improves your mood while counteracting any stress you experience. Engaging in any physical activities such as Yoga, Pilates, and Tai Chi helps rebalance and enhance the solar plexus chakra's energy. Ideally, spend some time in the warmth of the morning sun to further recharge the energy of the solar plexus chakra. Spending as little as 15 minutes in the early morning sun gives your body its daily dose of vitamin D. When your morning is off to a good start, this positivity usually stays with you throughout the day.

Unconditional Love

There are a lot of misconceptions about love. Most of us believe love is just an emotion we feel for others. Well, love is not only restricted to this, but it needs to be diverted toward yourself too. Self-love is as important as loving others. Another misconception about love is it is only about giving. To live a healthy, happy, and peaceful life, you need to be open to both receiving and giving love. If all you do is give, you will be left with nothing in the end for yourself. To help repair your heart chakra's energy, practice compassion, kindness, and love towards others and yourself. Once you understand what unconditional love feels like, it will automatically improve how you feel. It also fills you with plenty of positive emotions that instantly improve your mood. As you go through life, it's not only important to keep an open mind, but an open heart too.

Learn To Express Your Truth

All animals communicate in one form or another. Humans have an elaborate means of communication that includes verbal and nonverbal aspects such as body posture and gestures. We are quite lucky that we have a language for expressing ourselves. To recharge the energy of the throat chakra, you need to concentrate on expressing your truth. If you are not certain what that means, take some time for self-introspection and determine your core values. Examples of core values include compassion, kindness, timeliness, satisfaction, commitment, faith, hope, strength, courage, and so on. Anything dear to you is a core value. Now, it's time to determine whether you are living in sync with these core values or not. If you realize you're not, start making a few changes.

Even a simple act of saying no when your boundaries are violated or standing up for yourself helps recharge the throat chakra's energy. Similarly, you can start maintaining a journal to make a note of everything you feel and experience. Expressing your truth doesn't always have to be verbal. Even writing helps recharge the throat chakra's energy. Other simple techniques you can use for recharging its energy are singing, reading out loud, and communicating what you feel.

Work On Your Intuition

Were you ever in a situation when a little voice in your head told you not to do something or that you are in danger? Or perhaps it suggested an alternative course? If you have experienced this, it is your intuition trying to talk to you. We all have an instinct or a gut feeling about situations, people, and circumstances. Unfortunately, most of us ignore this little voice. To strengthen and revitalize the energy of the third eye chakra, you need to concentrate on your intuition. Listen to this little voice in your head. It is designed to help you make the right decisions and stay safe. Use your inner voice to act as a guiding force in life. By concentrating and improving your intuition, the energy of this chakra automatically elevates. Start paying attention to how you feel in certain situations. If the alarm bells start ringing, remove yourself from those situations and take a different course of action.

Connect With Your Spirit

An important aspect of life we often forget about is spirituality. Most believe spirituality is synonymous with religion. However, you can be spiritual without adhering to a specific religion. Whether you are religious or not is a personal choice. Spirituality is important for your well-being. It helps you see the big picture and identify your life's purpose. We all have a specific purpose, and we play a small role in life's bigger picture. Understanding your role, determining your life path, and working on it will bring a sense of personal satisfaction and peace that cannot be taken away. Spirituality also helps you to escape the chaos of life.

Reframe Your Beliefs

At times, a simple reason why the chakras are not working as intended is because of your current state of mind. If you are a pessimist and are constantly worrying about everything that can go wrong, you are attracting more negativity in your life. When your chakras are flooded with such negative energies, how can they function properly? If you want to take care of your chakras, it is time to reframe your beliefs. Believe it or not, people are often their own worst enemy and harshest critic. Your mindset matters a lot in life. Whether it is your mindset about dealing with fears, overcoming failure, or success, attitude cannot be overlooked. With a positive attitude, everything seems doable, while a negative attitude prevents you from taking the first step itself. Changing your mindset also improves your self-confidence and self-esteem. Reframing your beliefs makes you more aware of your thoughts and emotions about yourself and life in general. Self-reflection is an important part of growing. Unless you reflect upon your experiences, you cannot learn from them. If you don't learn from your mistakes, you will be doomed to repeat them and won't grow or progress in life.

A commonality between all the different techniques discussed in this section is the need for mindfulness. Mindfulness is a simple technique that helps you live in the moment without getting overwhelmed by thoughts of the past or future. What has happened cannot be undone, and what will happen cannot be predicted with certainty. Spending any time thinking about either of these scenarios leads to wastage of this precious resource. Instead, learn to live your life at the moment. The present is all you have, and learning to make the most of it is important for attaining your goals and objectives.

Chakra-Healing Foods

Everything in this universe is made of energy, and this includes the food you eat. What you eat matters because your body obtains the nourishment it needs from the food consumed. This is one of the reasons why you need to consume a healthy and wholesome diet. Unless you give your body all the nutrients it needs, it cannot function optimally.

The energy of different foods can affect the chakra's functioning. Chakras become blocked, don't spin vibrantly, or are closed due to energy imbalances. In all these instances, the flow of energy in your body is compromised. Always remember you are what you eat. How you feel, think, and your performance is all dependent on the food you eat. Food can be used as a healing and preventive measure to reduce the risk of illnesses.

If you are interested in balancing your chakras and increasing their energy, here are the different foods that are associated with the different chakras:

The Root Chakra

The root chakra is associated with the color red. As such, consuming foods that are red or have a red tinge will improve the energy of this chakra. The most common foods you can add to your diet are raspberries, strawberries, pomegranates, beetroots, tomatoes, and apples. The root chakra has a grounding effect on the body, and consuming foods grown inside the earth helps.

These vegetables, especially those mentioned above, are rich in antioxidants, beta-carotene, and vitamin C. You can add healthy root vegetables to your diet, including turmeric, carrots, sweet potatoes, parsnip, garlic, ginger, beets, onions, and sweet potatoes. Certain protein-rich foods such as lean cuts of meat, eggs, nuts, and beans can also help rebalance the root chakra's energy. Some spices associated with this chakra are cayenne pepper, paprika, and horseradish.

The Sacral Chakra

The second chakra is associated with the color orange. All foods that have an orange tinge can help balance the energy of this chakra. Some ingredients you can add to your daily diet are oranges, peaches, sweet potatoes, mangoes, carrots, papayas, and pears. All foods rich in Omega 3 fatty acids such as salmon, trout, and other naturally fatty fish can also work well. Similarly, sesame seeds, almonds, flaxseed, and walnuts are rich in Omega 3 fatty acids. These fatty acids help reduce inflammation and improve your cardiovascular health. Coconut, coconut water, and coconut oil also help rebalance this chakra's energy because it is associated with the element of water. The best spice for this chakra is cinnamon.

The Solar Plexus Chakra

The solar plexus chakra is associated with the color yellow. All yellow foods will help to rebalance the solar plexus chakra, such as pineapple, corn, lemon, lime, sweet lime, mangoes, and bananas. Consuming complex carbs and whole grains such as sprouted grains, spelt, brown rice, oats, rye, farro, and dietary fiber-rich vegetables also help to maintain this chakra's energy. Adding these helpful ingredients to your daily diet gives your body the essential dietary fiber it needs to function efficiently. It also creates a sustainable source of fuel to improve your overall energy levels.

The Heart Chakra

The heart chakra is associated with the color green. All foods that are green in color will help balance it. The first thing that you need to do is start adding plenty of dark leafy green vegetables to your diets, such as spinach, kale, Swiss Chard, lettuce, dandelion greens, celery, and parsley. All green vegetables and fruit, including cucumber, zucchini, peas, Kiwi, spirulina, sugar snap peas, green apples, and so on, will help. You can also drink green tea to help rebalance the energy of this chakra. If you want to start your day on a good note and give your body the essential ingredients it needs, consider having a green juice or a salad in the morning.

The Throat Chakra

The throat chakra is associated with the color blue, and all blue foods will help rebalance its energy. When you think of blue foods, consider blackberries, blueberries, and purple potatoes. All these foods are rich in antioxidants, vitamins, and dietary fiber your body needs. These are also great examples of complex carbohydrates essential for maintaining your energy levels. The healing and soothing food and liquids for this chakra also include raw honey, herbal teas, and coconut water. All fruit that is grown on trees such as apples, kiwi, plums, and pears can further heal the energy of the throat chakra.

The Third Eye Chakra

The energy of the third eye chakra is associated with the color purple. Purple grapes, eggplants, purple carrots, and purple kale help rebalance the energy of this chakra. These ingredients are rich in flavonoids and increase the production of serotonin that reduces stress and inflammation. Whenever you are stressed, a hormone known as cortisol is produced in your body. Serotonin helps counteract the harmful effects of this stress hormone. Another helpful ingredient you can add to your daily diet is cacao.

The Crown Chakra

The crown chakra is not associated with food but is more about detoxing your body. You cannot be in touch with your spirituality if your physical body is constantly overwhelmed. To align your consciousness with that of the universe, you need to take a break from eating. So, practicing regular fasts and detoxing your body from the inside helps heal this chakra's energy. When all the other chakras in your body are balanced, the crown chakra will become balanced. It is not just your diet but taking a break from the diet is equally important.

Detoxing and fasting help increase your energy levels, clear your mind, and flush out all toxins accumulating inside. The best practices to strengthen this chakra are meditation and yoga. Meditation herbs you can use to balance the crown chakra's energy are juniper, sage, lavender, and frankincense.

A diet that incorporates the different healing foods associated with the chakras will improve your physical health. When you are physically healthy and fit, catering to your emotional and mental needs becomes easier. Regardless of all that you can and cannot control, diet is one aspect well within your control.

Chapter 8: Leveraging the Power of Meditation

Meditation is a simple practice of mindfulness that helps your mind focus only on a specific thought, action, or object, and trains your awareness and attention. It helps you to achieve emotional and mental clarity while reducing any stress you are experiencing. A common misconception is that meditation is a religious practice. Even though several religions and cultures across the globe use meditation, the idea of meditation is more about getting in touch with your spirituality than religion. Practice meditation daily, and it will help reduce any stress you experience while improving your attention, concentration, memory, and learning power. It helps calm your mind and make sense of the world inside and around you without getting caught up in the chaos.

Regardless of the chakra you want to work on, meditation helps them all. Even meditating for 5-10 minutes every day can work wonders for you. No, you don't have to spend hours meditating to attain its benefits. If you want to meditate, don't get overwhelmed, and instead, concentrate on doing it for just 5 minutes to begin with.

Before you start meditating, you need to find a quiet room. Ensure you are the only one in this room and that there are no distractions. For 5-10 minutes, ask others not to disturb you. If possible, keep all gadgets out of reach and do not let them enter the sacred space. This is your Zen den. If you are constantly distracted, you cannot meditate effectively.

Once you have the meditation room ready, you need to make yourself comfortable. You can either sit on a chair or lie on the floor. It is entirely up to you. If you are lying on the floor, ensure you don't use a yoga mat. Let your body connect with the earth or the ground. Practicing meditation outdoors further amplifies the benefits it offers. While sitting, ensure your feet are firmly planted on the ground while your body is relaxed. Place your hands on your thighs, relax your shoulders while keeping your back upright, and relax your muscles. Similarly, when you are lying down, keep your back properly aligned and your arms resting by your side with the palms facing downwards. Maintaining good posture is important for optimizing the benefits of meditation. Good posture promotes physical relaxation. By physically relaxing your body, it becomes easier to calm your mind and regulate your thoughts.

Now that you are ready, it's time to close your eyes. Closing your eyes helps fine-tune your concentration. It also eliminates the chances of getting distracted by other visual cues or happenings in your surroundings. Close your eyes and shift all your focus to your breathing. Concentrate only on your breath and nothing else. You need to give your mind some time to calm down. Remember, your brain is constantly thinking, and unless you shift its attention to something relaxing, it will not stop. Notice how air enters and exits your body. Breathe in slowly and deeply through your nose, and then exhale slowly through your nose. Take deep and relaxing breaths and experience the feeling of relaxation spreading through your body.

Take all the time you need to relax and calm your mind. If you're still feeling overwhelmed, concentrate on deep breathing for a while longer. You can set the pace of meditation. Once you are relaxed and feel ready to move further into meditation and work on your chakras, start by concentrating on the colors associated with the different chakras. Here is a brief recap of the colors associated with the chakras:

The root chakra is associated with red, sacral chakra with orange, solar plexus chakra with yellow, heart chakra with pink or green, the throat chakra with blue, the third eye chakra with violet or indigo, and the crown chakra with white or gold. You can either start with a specific chakra where you've noticed an imbalance or perform a general overall chakra healing.

The first step is to start with the root chakra. This is the first chakra located at the base of your spine. It is your connection to the world and others in life. While working with the root chakra, concentrate on meditation by focusing on the color red. Visualize a red ball of light at the physical location of your root chakra. As you breathe in, see that the ball is slowly becoming bigger and bigger. As the red ball of light is growing in size, feel all the imbalances in this chakra washing away. Meditate until you feel calm, and once it feels that this chakra's energy feels balanced, visualize the ball becoming smaller once again.

This brings us to the second chakra. Concentrate on the physical location of the sacral chakra right below your navel. This chakra is associated with your inner child, creativity, and innocence. While thinking about these positive traits, shift your attention to the color orange. Visualize a ball of orange, slowly absorbing all impurities and imbalances present within the sacral chakra. Your breath is purifying you from the inside and washing away all the undesirable energies. Concentrate only on this color until it envelops you. Once this light surrounds you, thank it for the positive effect it has on you, and then visualize it returning to its original size once again. Hold onto the positive feeling and move on to the next chakra.

Shift your attention now to the solar plexus chakra. This chakra is present right above your navel, and the color associated with it is yellow. So, begin to focus only on this beautiful color. Think of the warm rays of the sun or any other yellow object in your mind's eye. Concentrate only on this color and let it slowly engulf you. As it is engulfing you, visualize all the imbalances in this chakra going away with it. Meditate on accepting the healing energy of the yellow color while removing any disturbances present within.

This brings us to the heart chakra. It is linked to your emotions of love, openness, kindness, trust, and compassion. It is associated with the colors green and pink. Visualize the heart chakra as a green or pink center slowly growing in size. As this light grows and spreads, you are slowly being engulfed by it. Let this brilliant light shield you. Imagine it is taking away all the negative energies clouding your heart chakra. Let this light grow in size and shine brighter. Once you feel as though this chakra has been healed, allow that ball of light to shrink down to its starting size, and then move onto the next chakra.

Shift your attention to the base of your throat, where the throat chakra is located. A simple way to meditate on this chakra is by visualizing a bright blue light at the base of your throat. Imagine this blue light as a small ball slowly growing in size as you breathe in and out. With every breath, you are bathed by this chakra's purifying energy, which is removing any self-doubt present within. Concentrate only on the throat chakra.

This brings us to the third eye chakra located in the middle of your forehead. While breathing in and out, imagine a small ball of bright indigo or violet light at the center of your forehead. With every purifying breath, this ball is growing in size until it has engulfed your forehead. Let this light flow down to all the other chakras below and engulf your body as a whole. Feel this light welcoming positivity into your life while getting rid of all traces of negativity. Thank this light for guiding the way and helping you trust your intuition. Thank the universe for the guidance it is giving you, and let the light return to your third eye.

The final chakra is the crown chakra. It is associated with the color white. Focus only on pure white light and let it engulf your senses. Let this light flood your body on the inside and surround you. Visualize that it has created a shield that's protecting you from negative energies, while filling you with a sense of calm and positivity. Keep meditating until the white color has surrounded you and you feel a deep sense of calm.

If you want, you can use any of the positive affirmations discussed in the previous chapter to further enhance this meditative exercise's power. Giving your mind something to concentrate on reduces the chances of getting distracted, so focusing on a specific affirmation can be highly beneficial. Remember, there are no hard and fast rules when it comes to meditation. It is a personal experience. You can change it according to what feels right for you. Meditation is neither a race nor a competition. You don't have to feel bad if you are unable to meditate properly without getting distracted. Even experienced practitioners of meditation still battle with wandering thoughts and distractions. Don't get discouraged, but instead, keep working at it every day.

If you notice your mind wanders while meditating, a simple way to shift its focus and concentrate on the meditation is by focusing on your breathing. Concentrate only on how it feels when you inhale and exhale. This simple exercise will help calm your mind and reestablish control over your thoughts. You can also practice breathing exercises whenever you feel stressed or overwhelmed. Hold on to the positive feelings you experience during meditation. Whenever facing any uncertainty in life, call upon this reassuring feeling and let it guide the way.

Conclusion

Chakras are the energy centers in your body, starting at the base of the spine and extending to the crown of the head. They are divided into seven major chakras and several minor ones. Each of these chakras needs to work in harmony with others to ensure your overall well-being and health. In this book, you were introduced to everything you need to heal and balance your chakras. If something feels amiss in your life, chances are that you have a chakra imbalance.

Opening, balancing, and healing your chakras is quite easy. Even spending as little as 10-15 minutes daily engaging in the different practices discussed in this book will help. Taking care of your well-being is your responsibility, and it cannot be delegated to anyone else. By tapping into the energy of your chakras, your self-awareness also increases. Self-awareness is important to growing, developing, and overcoming any setbacks.

Now, it's time to start implementing the simple suggestions, techniques, and tips discussed in this book. Once you learn to rebalance the energy of the different chakras, they will spin vibrantly like they're supposed to. You can improve the overall quality of your life physically, mentally, and spiritually by tapping into the power of the chakras.

Thank you for taking the time to read this book. I hope you have enjoyed learning about the different chakras and how to heal them. I wish you the best of luck in your spiritual journey!

www.ingramcontent.com/pod-product-compliance
Lightning Source LLC
LaVergne TN
LVHW012058070526
838200LV00070BA/3254